OVERLAND TO CALIFORNIA
IN 1859
A Guide for Wagon Train Travelers

EMIGRANTS CROSSING THE PLAINS.

OVERLAND TO CALIFORNIA

IN 1859

A Guide For Wagon Train Travelers

Compiled and Edited
by

LOUIS M. BLOCH JR.

BLOCH AND COMPANY
CLEVELAND, OHIO

Library of Congress Catalog Card Number 83-71506
ISBN NO. 0-914276-04-2

Published by Bloch and Company
P.O. Box 18058, Cleveland, Ohio 44118

Printed in the United States of America
by Printing Associates, Chardon, Ohio

Typesetting by A-M Graphics, Painesville, Ohio

Bound by George W. Steffen Bookbinders, Inc., Cleveland, Ohio

This book is dedicated to those unsung heros and heroines, the horses, mules and oxen without whose efforts and sacrifices, the journeys across the continent by wagon trains would have been impossible.

Preface

The westward migration to California started in the 1840's. It was stimulated by the climate, by varied resources including timber, wild horses, fish, herds of elk, waterfoul and other wild game, and by the possibilities of agricultural wealth. Captain John Sutter and other settlers had found fertile land for wheat, vineyards and cattle grazing.

In March, 1848, gold was discovered on lands owned by John A. Sutter near Sacramento, California. By the middle of May, 1848, San Francisco was almost deserted by the rush to the gold fields. It was in September, 1848 that news of the discovery reached the East. When President Polk included the reports of gold in California in his December, 1848 message to Congress, the country was in a frenzy and the gold rush was on.

Soon sixty-one ships began the trip around South America to California. By April, 1849, thousands of wagons began the trip to California. People died of cholera, dysentery and fever. Most knew little of plains travel and little information was available.

It was not until ten years later in 1859 that Randolph B. Marcy, A Captain in the U.S. Army, decided to write *A Hand-Book For Overland Expeditions* with maps, illustrations and itineraries of the principal routes between the Mississippi and the Pacific. Captain Marcy believed that traveling the plains and mountains was an art that must be studied. He was convinced that many previous failures could have been prevented with adequate preparations in advance.

Most of this book consists of actual quotations from *The Prairie Traveler,* Captain Marcy's Handbook for Overland Expeditions published in 1859. We also quote from *Kanzas and Nebraska* by Edward Everett Hale, published in 1854, and *The Annals of San Francisco and The History of California* published in 1855 and *The States and Territories of The Great West* published in 1856. Prints and maps are from these four books. The cover print is from *Our New West* by Samuel Bowles, published in 1869, while the advertisements are reproduced from *The United States Commercial Register,* published in 1852. The original text is exactly quoted from these books, so some grammar, spelling and sentence construction varies slightly from present day standards. We elected not to change the original text.

CONTENTS

MAPS AND ILLUSTRATIONS

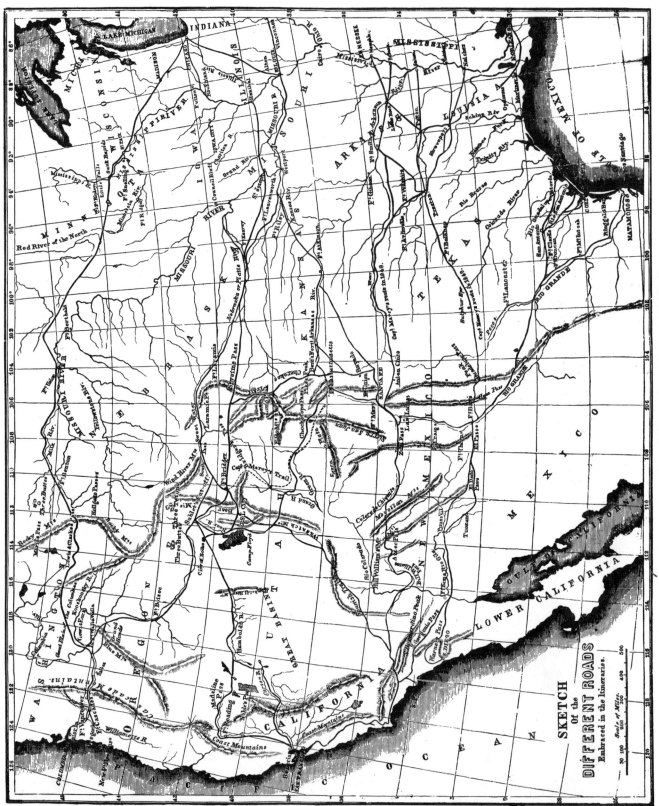

This map was published in 1859 for emigrants to California

SKETCH
of the
DIFFERENT ROADS
Embraced in the itineraries.

Choosing A Route
To California

Before we start on our overland trip to California in this year of 1859, many preparations must be made. The success of our journey and even our very lives may depend on the decisions we make. To help us to answer our many questions we consult *The Prairie Traveler,* a Hand-Book for Overland Expeditions, written in 1859 by Randolph B. Marcy, Captain of the U.S. Army. Captain Marcy had a quarter of a century's experience in frontier life and explored the interior of our continent where he was far from populated places. He had to depend entirely on his own resources to survive.

Our first decision is to choose a route to California. Looking at our map from *The Prairie Traveler,* we find that there are several routes that we can take to the West Coast.

At this point we quote from *The Prairie Traveler.*

"Persons living in the Northeastern States can reach the eastern terminus of any one of the routes they may select by public transport." The public transportation referred to is, of course, railroad and stagecoach transportation. *The Prairie Traveler* goes on to state, "As animals are much cheaper on the frontier than in the Eastern States, travelers should purchase their teams at or near the point where the overland journey is to commence.

"Those who live in the middle Western States, having their own means of transportation and going to any point on the Pacific Coast, should take one of the middle routes. Others, who live in the extreme Southwest, and whose destination is south of San Francisco, should travel the southern road running through Texas, which is the only one practicable for comfortable winter travel. The grass upon a great portion of this route is green during the entire winter, and snow seldom covers it. This road leaves the Gulf coast at Powder Horn, on Matagorda Bay, which point is difficult of access by land from the north, but may be reached by steamers from New Orleans five times a week. There are stores at Powder Horn and Indianola where the traveler can obtain most of the articles necessary for his journey, but I would recommend him to supply himself before leaving New Orleans with everything he requires with the exception of animals, which he will find cheaper in Texas. This road has received a large amount of travel since 1849, is well tracked and defined, and excepting about twenty miles of 'hog wallow prairie' near Powder Horn, it is an excellent road for carriages and wagons. It passes through a settled country for 250 miles, and within this section supplies can be had at reasonable rates. At Victoria and San Antonio many fine stores will be found, well supplied with stocks of goods, embracing all the articles the traveler will require.

"The next route to the north is that over which the semi-weekly mail to California passes, and which, for a great portion of the way to New Mexico, Capt. Marcy traveled in 1849. This road leaves the Arkansas River at Fort Smith, to which point steamers run during the seasons of high water in the winter and spring. Supplies of all descriptions necessary for the overland journey may be procured at Fort Smith. Horses and cattle are cheap here. The road on leaving Fort Smith passes through the Choctaw and Chickasaw country for 180 miles, then crosses the Red River by ferry-boat at Preston, and runs through the border settlements of northern Texas for 150 miles, within which distances supplies may be procured at moderate prices. This road is accessible to persons desiring to make the entire journey with their own transportation from Tennessee or Mississippi, by crossing the Mississippi River at Memphis or Helena, passing Little Rock and intersecting the road at Preston. This road also unites with the San Antonio road at El Paso, and from that point they pass together over the mountains to Fort Yuma and to San Francisco in California. This road, for the greater portion of the distance, is the same that has been since recommended for a Pacific railway. The grass upon all the roads leaving Fort Smith is sufficiently advanced to afford sustenance to animals by the first of April, and from this time until winter sets in it is abundant.

"The next route on the north leaves the Missouri River at Westport, Leavenworth City, Atcheson, or from other towns above, between either of which points and St. Louis steamers ply during the entire summer season.

"The necessary outfit of supplies can always be procured at any of the starting-points on the Missouri at moderate rates.

"This is the great emigrant route from Missouri to California and Oregon, over which so many thousands have traveled within the past few years. The track is broad, well worn, and cannot be mistaken. It has received the major part of the Mormon emigration, and was traversed by the army in its march to Utah in 1857. At the point where this road crosses the South Platte River, Lieutenant Bryan's road branches off to the left, leading through Bridger's Pass, and thence to Fort Bridger. From Fort Bridger there are two roads that may be traveled with wagons in the direction of California; one passing Salt Lake City, and the other running down Bear River to Soda Springs, intersecting the Salt Lake City road at the City of Rocks. Near Soda Springs the Oregon road turns to the right, passing Fort Hall, and thence down the Snake River to Fort Wallah-Wallah. Unless travelers have business in Salt Lake Valley, I would advise them to take the Bear River route, as it is much shorter, and better in every respect.

"Many persons who have had much experience in prairie traveling prefer leaving the Missouri River in March or April, and feeding grain to their animals until the new grass appears. The roads become muddy and heavy after the spring rains set in, and by starting out early the worst part of the road will be passed over before the ground becomes wet and soft. This plan, however, should never be attempted unless the animals are well supplied with grain, and kept in good condition. They will eat the old grass in the spring, but it does not, in this climate, as in Utah and New Mexico, afford them sufficient sustenance.

"The grass, after the 1st of May, is good and abundant upon this road as far as the South Pass, from whence there is a section of about 50 miles where it is scarce; there is also a scarcity upon the desert beyond the sink of the Humboldt. As large numbers of cattle pass over the road annually, they soon consume all the grass in these barren localities, and such as pass late in the season are likely to suffer greatly, and oftentimes perish from starvation. When I came over the road in August, 1858, I seldom found myself out of sight of dead cattle for 500 miles along the road, and this was an unusually favorable year for grass, and before the main body of animals had passed for the season."

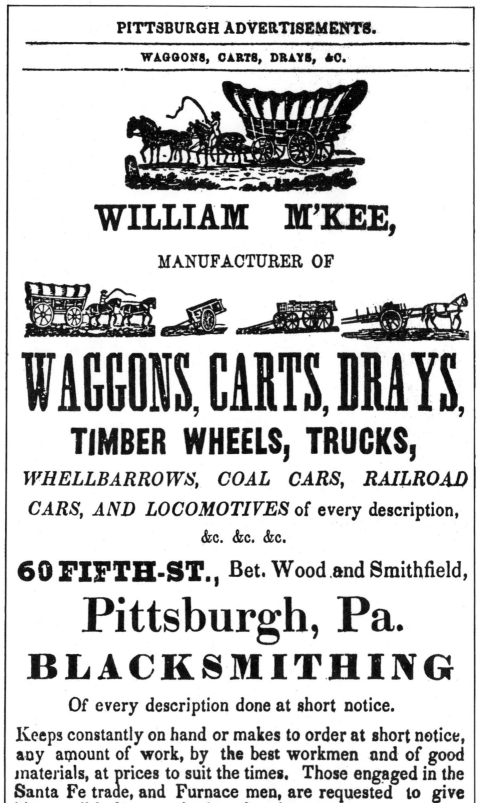

Organization of Companies

"After a particular route has been selected to make the journey across the plains, and the requisite number have arrived at the eastern terminus, their first business should be to organize themselves into a company and elect a commander. The company should be of sufficient magnitude to herd and guard animals, and for protection against Indians. From 50 to 70 men, properly armed and equipped will be enough for these purposes, and any greater number only makes the movements of the party more cumbersome.

"In the selection of a captain, good judgement, integrity of purpose, and practical experience are the essential requisites. His duty should be to direct the order of march, the time of starting and halting, to select the camps, detail and give orders to guards, and indeed, to control and superintend the movements of the company.

"An obligation should then be drawn up and signed by all the members of the association, wherein each one should bind himself to abide in all cases by the orders and decisions of the captain, and to aid him by every means in his power in the execution of his duties; and they should also obligate themselves to aid each other, so as to make the individual interest of each member the common concern of the whole company. To insure this, a fund should be raised for the purchase of extra animals to supply the places of those which may give out or die on the road; and if the wagon or team of a particular member should fail and have to be abandoned, the company should obligate themselves to transport his luggage. Thus it will be made the interest of every member of the company to watch over and protect the property of others as well as his own.

"In case of failure on the part of any one to comply with the obligations imposed by the articles of agreement, the company should have the power to punish the delinquent member, and, if necessary, to exclude him from all the benefits of the association.

"On such a journey as this, there is much to interest and amuse on who is fond of picturesque scenery, and of wild life in its most primitive aspect, yet no one should attempt it without anticipating many rough knocks and much hard labor; every man must expect to do his share of duty faithfully and without a murmer.

"On long and arduous expeditions men are apt to become irritable and ill-natured, and oftentimes fancy they have more labor imposed upon them than their comrades, and that the person who directs the march is partial toward his favorites, etc. That man who exercises the greatest forbearance under such circumstances, who is cheerful, slow to take up quarrels, and endeavors to reconcile difficulties among his companions, is deserving of all praise, and will, without doubt, contribute largely to the success and comfort of an expedition.

"The advantages of an association such as I have mentioned are numerous. The animals can be herded together and guarded by the different members of the company in rotation, thereby securing to all the opportunities of sleep and rest. Besides, this is the only way to resist attacks of the Indians, and to prevent their stampeding and driving off animals; and much more efficiency is secured in every respect, especially in crossing streams, repairing roads, etc. Unless a systematic organization be adopted, it is impossible for a party of any size to travel in company for any great length of time, and for all the members to agree upon the same arrangements in marching, camping, etc. When a captain has once been chosen, he should be sustained in all his decisions unless he commit some manifest outrage, at which time a majority of the company can remove him and put a better man in his place.

"A company having been organized, its first interest is to procure a proper outfit of transportation and supplies for the contemplated journey. Wagons should be of the simplest possible construction— strong, light and made of well-seasoned timber, especially the wheels, as the atmosphere, in the elevated and arid region over which they have to pass, is so exceedingly dry during the summer months, that, unless the wood-work is thoroughly seasoned, they will require constant repairs to prevent them from falling to pieces. Wheels made of Osage orangewood, are the best for the plains, as they shrink but little, and seldom want repairing. As, however, this wood is not easily procured in the Northern States, white oak answers a very good purpose if well seasoned.

"Spring wagons made in Concord, New Hampshire, are used to transport passengers and the mails upon some of the routes across the plains, and they are said, by those who have used them, to be much superior to any others. They are made of the close-grained oak that grows in a high northern latitude, and well seasoned.

"One of the chief causes of accidents to carriages upon the plains arises from the nuts coming off from the numerous bolts that secure the running gearing. To prevent this, the ends of all the bolts should be riveted; it is seldom necessary to take them off, and when this is required, the ends of the bolts may easily be filed away.

"Wagons with six mules should never, on a long journey over the prairies, be loaded with over 2,000 pounds, unless grain is transported, when an additional 1,000 pounds may be taken, provided it is fed out daily to the team. When grass constitutes the only forage, 2,000 pounds is deemed a suffficient load. Every wagon should be furnished with substantial bows and double covers, to protect its contents from the sun and weather.

"There has been much discussion regarding the relative merits of mules and oxen for prairie traveling, and the question is yet far from being settled. Upon good firm roads, in a populated country, where grain can be procured, I should unquestionably give the preference to mules, as they travel faster, and endure the heat of summer much better than oxen; and if the journey be not over 1,000 miles, and the grass abundant, even without grain, I think mules would be preferable. But when the march is to extend 1,500 or 2,000 miles, or over a rough sandy or muddy road, I believe young oxen will endure better than mules. Besides, they are much more economical, a team of six mules costing six hundred dollars, while an eight-ox team only costs upon the frontier about two hundred dollars. Oxen are much less liable to be stampeded and driven off by Indians, and can be pursued and overtaken by horsemen; and finally, they can, if necessary be used for beef.

"Ox traveling, when once a man becomes accustomed to it, is not so disagreeable as might be expected, particularly if one succeeds in obtaining a tractable animal. In emergencies, an ox can be made to proceed at a tolerable quick pace; for though his walk is only about three miles an hour at an average, he may be made to perform double that distance in the same time.

"Cows will be found very useful upon long journeys when the rate of travel is slow, as they furnish milk, and in emergencies they may be worked in wagons."

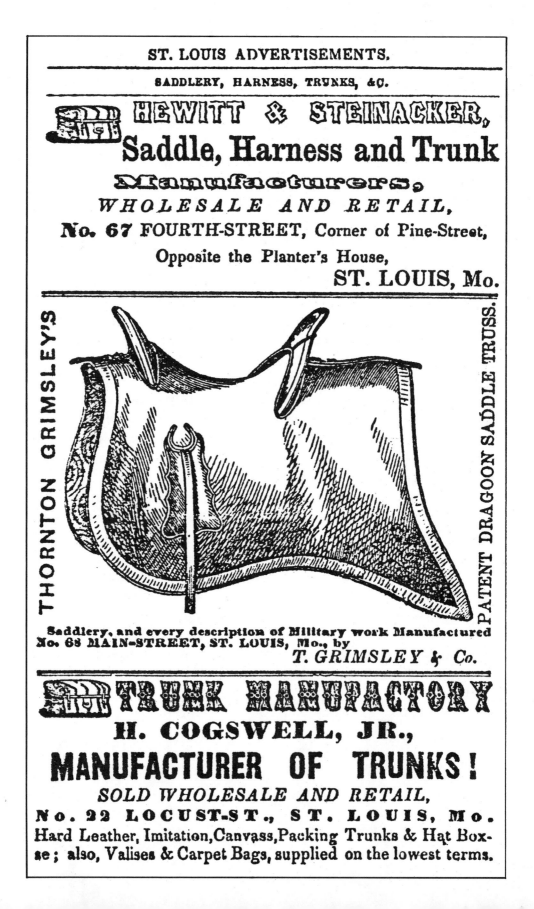

Supplies and Provisions

"On your trip to California your selection of supplies is of the greatest importance. These supplies should be put up in the most secure, compact and portable shape. Bacon should be packed in strong sacks of a hundred pounds to each; or, in very hot climates, put in boxes and surrounded with bran, which, in a great measure, prevents the fat from melting away. If pork is used, in order to avoid transporting about forty percent of useless weight, it should be taken out of the barrels and packed like bacon; then so placed in the bottom of the wagons as to keep it cool. The pork, if well cured, will keep several months in this way, but bacon is preferable. Flour should be packed in stout double canvas sacks well sewed, a hundred pounds in each sack. Butter may be preserved by boiling it thoroughly and skimming off the scum as it rises to the top until it is quite clear like oil. It is then placed in tin canisters and soldered up. This mode of preserving butter has been adopted in the hot climate of southern Texas, and it is found to keep sweet for a great length of time, and its flavor is but little impared by the process. Sugar may be well secured in india-rubber sacks, or so placed in the wagon as not to risk getting wet. Dried vegetables are almost equal to the fresh, and are put up in such a compact and portable form as easily to be transported over the plains. These dried vegetables are prepared by cutting them into thin slices and subjecting them to a very powerful press, which removes the juice and leaves a solid cake, which, after having been thoroughly dried in an oven, becomes almost as hard as a rock. A small piece of this, about the size of a man's hand, when boiled, swells up so as to fill a vegetable dish, and is sufficient for four men. Canned vegetables are very good, but not so portable as when put up in the other form."

Clothing

"A suitable dress for prairie traveling is of great importance to health and comfort. Cotton or linen fabrics do not sufficiently protect the body against the direct rays of the sun at midday, nor against rains or sudden changes of temperature. Wool, being a nonconductor, is the best material for this mode of locomotion, and should always be adopted for the plains. The coat should be short and stout, the shirt of red or blue flannel, such as can be found in almost all the shops on the frontier; this, in warm weather, answers for an outside garment. The pants should be of thick and soft woolen material, and it is well to have them re-enforced on the inside, where they come in contact with the saddle, with soft buckskin, which makes them more durable and comfortable. Woolen socks and stout boots, coming up well at the knees, and made large, so as to admit the pants, will be found the best for horsemen, and they guard against rattlesnake bites.

"In traveling through deep snow during very cold weather in winter, moccasins are preferable to boots or shoes, as being more pliable, and allowing a freer circulation of the blood. To repair shoes an awl with buckskin strings is used. They should never be forgotten in making up the outfit for a prairie expedition.

Camp Equipage

"The bedding for each person should consist of two blankets, a comforter, and a pillow, and a painted canvas cloth to spread beneath the bed upon the ground, and to contain it when rolled up for transportation.

"Every mess of six or eight persons will require a wrought-iron camp kettle, large enough for boiling meat and making soup; a coffee pot and cups of heavy tin, tin plates, frying and bake pans of wrought iron, the latter for baking bread and roasting coffee, knives, forks, and spoons, a bucket, an axe, hatchet and spade. Matches should be carried in bottles and corked tight, so as to exclude the moisture. Quinine, opium and some cathartic medicine.

"The following list of articles is deemed a sufficient outfit for one man upon a three month's expedition:

2 blue or red flannel overshirts
2 woolen undershirts
2 pairs thick cotton drawers
4 pairs woolen socks
2 pairs cotton socks
4 colored silk handkerchiefs
2 pairs stout shoes, for footmen
1 pair boots, for horsemen
1 pair shoes, for horsemen
1 poncho
1 coat and 1 overcoat

1 comb and brush
2 tooth-brushes
1 pound castile soap
3 pounds bar soap for
    washing clothes
1 belt-knife & whetstone
Stout linen thread, large needles,
    a bit of beeswax, a few buttons,
    paper of pins, and a thimble, all
    contained in a small buckskin or
    or cloth bag.

20

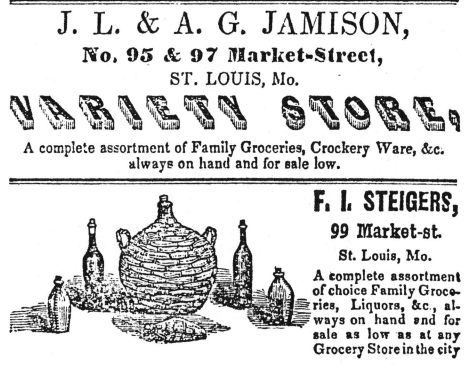

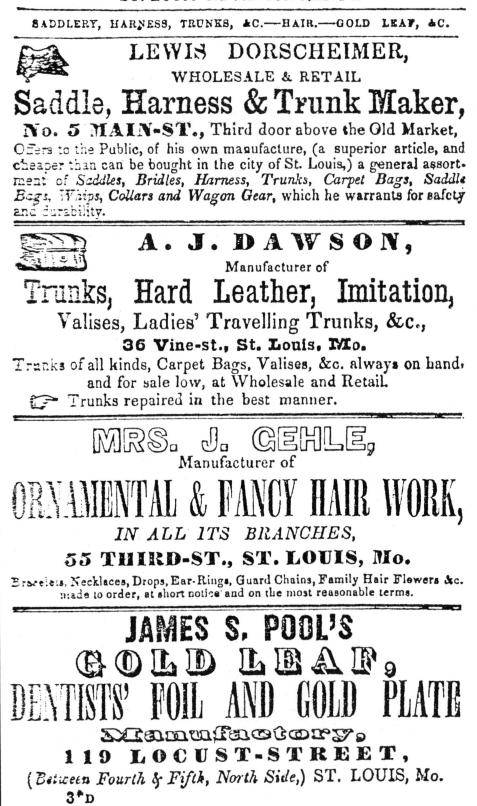

"In outfitting their wagons men are very prone to overload their teams with a great variety of useless articles. It is a good rule to carry nothing more than is absolutely necessary for use upon the journey. One can not expect, with the limited allowance of transportation that emigrants usually have, to indulge in luxuries upon such expeditions, articles for use in California can be purchased there at less cost than that of overland transportation.

"I would advise all persons who travel for any considerable time through a country where they can procure no vegetables to carry with them some essence of lemon as a prevention for scurvy.

"The allowance of provisions for each grown person, to make the journey from the Missouri River to California, should suffice for 110 days. The following is deemed necessary; 150 lbs. of flour, or its equivalent in hard bread; 25 lbs. of bacon or pork, and enough fresh beef to be driven on the hoof to make up the meat component of the diet; 15 lbs. of coffee and 25 lbs. of sugar;also a quantity of yeast powders for making bread, and salt & pepper. These are the chief articles of subsistence necessary for the trip, and they should be used with economy, reserving a good portion for the western half of the journey. Heretofore many of the California emigrants have exhausted their stocks of provisions before reaching their journey's end, and have, in many cases, been obliged to pay the most exorbitant prices in making up the deficiency. It is true that if persons choose to pass through Salt Lake City, and the Mormons happen to be in an amiable mood, supplies may sometimes be procured from them; but those who have visited them well know little reliance is to be placed upon their hospitality or spirit of accomodation.

"Every man who goes into the Indian country should be armed with a rifle and a revolver, and he should never, either in camp or out of it, lose sight of them. When not on the march, they should be placed in such a position that they can be seized at an instant's warning; and when moving about outside the camp, the revolver should be worn in the belt, as the person does not know at what moment he may have use for it. Colt's revolving pistol is very generally admitted, both in Europe and America, to be the most efficient arm of its kind known at the present day."

HALF-FACED CAMP

CONICAL BIVOUAC

Camping

"In traveling with pack animals it is not always convenient or practicable to transport tents, and the travelers ingenuity is often taxed in devising the most available means for making himself comfortable and secure against winds and storms. I have been astonished to see how soon an experienced voyager, without any resources save those provided by nature, will erect a comfortable shelter in a place where a person having no knowledge of woodcraft would never think of such a thing.

"Almost all people in different parts of the world have their own peculiar methods of camping. In the severe climate of Tibet they encamp near large rocks, which adsorb the heat during the day, and give it out slowly during the night. They form, as it were, reservoirs of calories.

"In the polar regions the Eskimos live and make themselves comfortable in huts of ice or snow, and with no other combustible but oil. The natives of Australia bury their bodies in the sand, keeping their heads only above the surface, and thus sleep warm during the chilly nights of that climate.

"Fortunately for the health and comfort of travelers upon the Plains, the atmosphere is pure and dry during the greater part of the year, and it is seldom that any rain or dew is seen. The night air of the summer months is soft, exhilarating, and delightful. Persons may therefore sleep in it and inhale it with perfect umpunity, and, indeed many prefer this to breathing the confined atmosphere of a tent. During the rainy season only is it necessary to seek shelter. In traveling with covered wagons one always has protection from storms, but with pack trains it becomes necessary to improvise the best substitutes for tents.

"A very secure protection against storms may be constructed by planting firmly in the ground two upright poles, with forks at their tops, and crossing them with a light pole laid in the forks. A sheet of canvas may be attached by one side to the horizontal pole, the opposite edge being stretched out to the windward at an angle of about forty-five degrees to the ground, and there fastened with wooden pins, or with buckskin strings tied to the lower border of the canvas and to pegs driven firmly into the earth. This forms a shelter

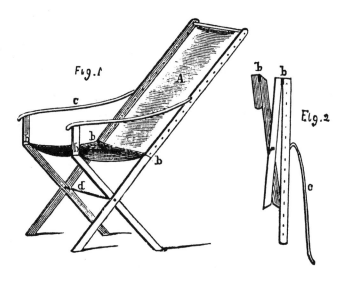

CAMP CHAIR NO. 1

CAMP CHAIRS NOS. 2 AND 3

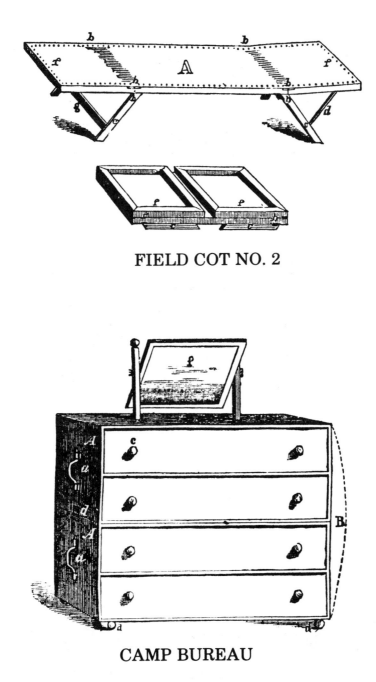

FIELD COT NO. 2

CAMP BUREAU

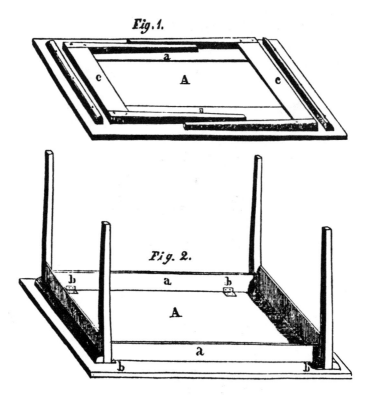

Fig. 1.

Fig. 2.

CAMP TABLE

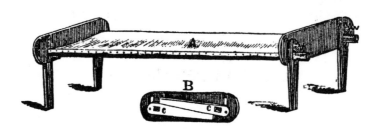

FIELD COT NO. 1

for three or four men, and is a good defense against winds and rains. If a fire be then made in front, the smoke will be carried away, so as not to incommode the occupants of the tent. This is called a "half-faced" camp.

"Another method practiced a great deal among mountain men and Indians consists in placing several rough poles equidistant around in a half circle, and bringing the small ends together at the top, where they are bound with a thong. This forms the conical frame-work of the tent, which when covered with a cloth stretched around it, makes a very good shelter, and is preferable to the half faced tent, because the sides are covered. When no cloths, blankets, or hides are at hand to be placed over the poles of the lodge, it may be covered with green boughs laid on compactly, so as to shed a good deal of rain, and keep out the wind in cold weather.

Camp Furniture

"The accompanying illustrations present some convenient articles of portable camp furniture.

CAMP CHAIR No. 1 is of oak or other hard wood. Fig. 1 represents it opened for use; in Fig. 2 it is closed for transportation.

A is a stout canvas, forming the back and seat; b,b,b are iron butt-hinges; c,c are leather straps, one inch and a quarter wide, forming the arms; d is an iron rod, with nut and screw at one end.

CAMP CHAIR No. 2 is made of sticks tied together with thongs of buckskin or raw hide.

CAMP CHAIR No. 3 is a very comfortable seat, made of a barrel, the part forming the seat being filled with grass.

CAMP TABLE. *Fig. 1* represents the table folded for transportation; in *Fig. 2* it is spread out for use. A is the top of the table; a,a are side boards and c,c are end boards, turning on butt-hinges, b,b,b.

FIELD COTS. No. 1 represents the cot put up for use; B, the cot folded for transportation. The legs turn upon iron bolts running through the head and foot boards; they are then placed upon the canvas, and the whole is rolled up around the side pieces. In No. 2 the upper figure represents the cot put up for use; the lower shows it folded for transportation. A is a stout canvas; b,b are iron butt-hinges; c,c, the legs; d,d, leather straps, with buckels, which hold the legs firm; *f,f*, ends, which fold upon hinges; *g,g*, cross-bars from leg to leg. This cot is strong, light and portable.

CAMP BUREAU. This cut represents two chests, *A,A*, with their handles, *a,a;* the covers taken off, they are placed one upon the other, and secured by the clamps *B,B; d* shows the division between the two chests. When it is to be transported, the knobs, *c*, are unscrewed from the drawers, the looking-glass, *f,* is removed, the drawers are filled with clothing, etc., and the lids are screwed on.

MESS-CHEST. *A* represents the chest open for table; *B* is the same closed; *C* is the upper tray of tin, with compartments, *b,b; E* is the lower wooden tray, divided into compartments, *a,a,* for various purposes, and made fast to the bottom of the chest; *d,d* are lids opening with hinges; *f* (in figure *B*) is a wooden leg, turning upon a hinge, and fitting snugly between two pieces of wood screwed upon the cover."

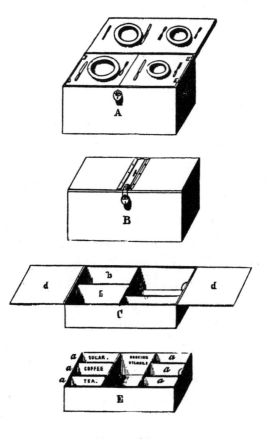

MESS-CHEST

30

Litters

"Should a party traveling with pack animals, and without ambulances or wagons, have one of its members wounded or taken so sick as to be unable to walk or ride on horseback, a litter may be constructed by taking two poles about twenty feet in length, uniting them by two sticks three feet long lashed across the centre at six feet apart, and stretching a piece of stout canvas, a blanket, or hide between them to form the bed. Two steady horses or mules are then selected, placed between the poles in the front and rear of the litter, and the ends of the poles made fast to the sides of the animals, either by attachment to the stirrups or to the ends of straps secured over their backs.

"The patient may then be placed upon the litter, and is ready for the march."

HORSE-LITTER

MORMONS EMIGRATING TO UTAH IN 1847.

J. W. ORR N.Y.

Marching

"The success of a long expedition through an unpopulated country depends mainly on the care taken of the animals, and the manner in which they are driven, herded and guarded. If they are broken down or lost, everything must be sacrificed, and the party becomes perfectly helpless.

"The great error into which inexperienced travelers are liable to fall, and which brings more suffering and disaster than almost anything else, lies in overworking their cattle at the beginning of the journey. To overcome this, short and easy drives should be made until the teams become accustomed to their work. If animals are overloaded and overworked when they first start out into the prairies, they soon fall away and give out before reaching the end of the journey.

"Grass and water are abundant and good upon the eastern portions of all the different overland routes; animals should not, therefore, with proper care, give out in the least before reaching the mountains. West of the mountains water and grass are scarce and animals must be in the best condition to endure that part of the journey. Drivers should be closely watched, and never, unless absolutely necessary, be permitted to beat their animals, or to force them out of a walk, as this will soon break their animals. Those teamsters who make the least use of the whip invariably keep their animals in the best condition.

"In traveling with ox teams in this summer season, great benefit will be derived from making early marches; starting with the dawn, and making a "nooning" during the heat of the day, as oxen suffer much from the heat of the sun in midsummer. These noon halts should, if possible, be so arranged as to be near grass and water. When it gets cool they may be hitched to the wagons again, and the journey continued in the afternoon. Sixteen or eighteen miles a day may be made without injury to the animals, and longer drives are not advised, unless in order to reach grass and water.

"The scarcity of water upon some of the routes across the plains occasionally exposes the traveler to intense suffering. In mountainous districts water can generally be found either in springs, the dry beds of streams, or in holes in the rocks. During a season of the year when there are occasional showers, water will generally be found in low places where there is clay, but after the dry season has set in these pools evaporate, and it is necessary to dig wells. The lowest spots should be selected for this purpose when the grass is green and the surface earth moist. In searching for water along the dry sandy beds of streams, it is well to try the earth with a stick, and if this shows moisture, water will generally be obtained by digging. It is a rule with prairie travelers, in searching for water in a sandy country, to ascend the streams, and the nearer their sources are approached, the more water will be found in a dry season. There are many indications of water known to old campaigners. The most certain of them are deep green cottonwood or willow trees growing in low country; also flags, water-rushes, tall green grass, etc. The fresh tracks and trails of animals converging toward a common center, and the flight of birds and water-fowl toward the same points, will also lead to water. In a section with many deer, it may be certain that water is not far distant, as these animals drink daily, and they will not remain long in a locality after the water has dried up. Deer generally go to water during the middle of the day, but birds toward evening.

"A supply of drinking water may be obtained during a shower from the drippings of a tent, or by suspending a cloth or blanket by the four corners and hanging a small weight at the center, so as to allow all the rain to run toward one point, from whence it drops into a vessel beneath. Painted canvas cloths answer a very good purpose for catching water during a rain, but they should be previously well washed, to prevent them from imparting a bad taste. When there are heavy dews, water may be collected by spreading out a blanket, dragging it over the grass, and wringing out the water it collects. Water taken from stagnant pools should be thoroughly boiled, and all the scum removed from the surface as it rises; also mixing powdered charcoal helps to disinfect the water. Water may also be purified by placing a piece of alum in the end of a stick that has been split, and stirring it around in a bucket of water. To cool water wrap cloths around the vessel containing it, wet them and hang in the air, where a rapid evaporation will be produced."

Journadas

"In some localities 50 or 60 miles, and even greater distances, are frequently traversed without water; these long stretches are called by the Mexicans "Journadas" or day's journey. There is one in New Mexico called "Journada del Muerto", which is 78½ miles in length, where in a dry season, there is not a drop of water; yet with the proper care, this drive can be made with ox or mule teams, and without loss or injury to the animals.

"On arriving at the last camping-ground before entering upon the journada, all the animals should be as well rested and refreshed as possible. To insure this, they must be turned out upon the best grass that can be found, and allowed to eat and drink as much as they desire during the entire halt. Should the weather be very warm, and the teams composed of oxen, the march should not be resumed until it begins to cool in the afternoon. They should be carefully watered just previous to being hitched up and started out upon the journada, the water-kegs having been previously filled. The drive is then commenced, and continued during the entire night, with 10 or 15 minutes rest every two hours. About daylight a halt should be made, and the animals immediately turned out to graze for two hours, during which time, especially if there is dew upon the grass, they will have become considerably refreshed, and may be put to the wagon again and driving until the heat becomes oppressive toward noon, when they are again turned out upon a spot where the grass is good, and, if possible where there are shade trees. About four o'clock P.M. they are again started, and the march continued into the night, as long as they can be driven without suffering. If, however, there should be dew, which is seldom the case on the plains, it would be well to turn out the animals several times during the second night, and by morning, if they are in good condition, the journada of 70 or 80 miles will have been passed without any great amount of suffering.

"Oxen upon a long journey will sometimes wear down their hoofs and become lame. When this occurs, a thick piece of raw hide wrapped around the foot and tied firmly to the leg will solve the difficulty, providing the weather is not wet. Mexican and Indian horses and mules will make long journeys without being shod, as their hoofs are tough and elastic, and wear away very gradually."

CROSSING A STREAM

SWIMMING A HORSE

Advance and Rear Guards, Camps, Fording Rivers

"A few men, well mounted, should constitute the advance and rear guards for each train of wagons passing through Indian country. Their duty will be to keep a look-out in all directions, and to search places where Indians would be likely to lie in ambush. Should hostile Indians be discovered, the fact should be at once reported to the commander, who, if he anticipates an attack, will rapidly form his wagons into a circle or "corral" with the animals toward the center, and the men on the inside, with their arms in readiness to repel an attack. If these arrangements are properly handled, a few parties of Indians will make an attack, as they are well aware that some of their warriors might pay with their lives.

Selection of Camps

"The security of animals, and indeed, the general safety of a party, in traveling through a country occupied by hostile Indians, depends greatly upon the selection of camps. One of the most important considerations that should influence the choice of a locality is its capability for defense. It is advisable to select a position in which one or more sides of the camp shall rest upon the crest of a hill or bluff. The prairie Indians make their camps upon the summits of the hills, whence they can see in all directions, and thus avoid a surprise. Picket guards should be stationed at points two or three hundred yards from the camp, on low ground so that an enemy approaching over the surrounding higher country can be seen against the sky, while the guard is screened from observation. These sentinels should not be allowed to keep fires. During the day the picket guards should be posted on the highest ground near the camp to keep a look-out in all directions and if not within hailing distance, they should be instructed to give some signal to inform those in camp of danger. Should the pickets suddenly discover a party of Indians very near, and with the intention of making an attack, they should fire their pieces to give the alarm to the camp. It is of utmost importance that picket guards should be wide awake, and allow nothing to escape their observation, as the safety of the whole camp is involved. During a dark night a man can see better himself, and is less exposed to the view of others, when in a sitting position than when standing up or moving about. Horses and mules, whose senses of hearing and smelling are probably more acute than those of almost any other animals, will discover anything strange or unusual about camp much sooner than a man. They indicate this by turning in the direction from whence the object is approaching, holding their heads erect, projecting their ears forward, and standing in a fixed and attentive attitude. They exhibit the same signs of alarm when a wolf or other wild animal approaches the camp; but it is always wise, when they show fear in this manner, to be on the alert till the cause is determined. Mules are very keenly sensitive to danger, and, in passing along over the prairies, they will often detect strangers long before they are discovered by their riders. Nothing seems to escape their observation; and I have heard of several instances where they have given timely notice of the approach of hostile Indians, and thus prevented stampedes. Dogs are sometimes good sentinels, but they often sleep soundly, and are not easily awakened on the approach of an enemy.

"In marching with a large force, unless there is a guide who knows the country, a small party should always be sent in advance to search for good camping places. A party should average upon the prairies, where the roads are good, about 18 miles a day, but, if necessary, it can make 25 or even 30 miles. When a halt is made the wagons are "corraled", as it is called, by bringing the two front ones near and parallel to each other. The two next are then driven up on the outside of these, with the front wheels of the first wagons touching the rear wheels of these next two. This method is continued until a half circle is made. Then the other half circle is made to close the "corral". An opening of about twenty yards should be left between the last two wagons for animals to pass in and out of the "corral", and this may be closed with two ropes streched between the wagons. Such a "corral" forms an excellent and secure barricade against Indian attacks, and a good enclosure for cattle while they are being yolked.

Enclosures are made in the same manner for horses and mules, and in case of an attempt to stampede them, they should be driven with all possible haste into the "corral", where they will be perfectly safe. A stampede is more to be dreaded upon the plains than almost any disaster that can happen. It sometimes happens that many animals are lost in this way. The Indians are familiar with the habits of horses and mules and the best ways to stampede them. Previous to attempting a stampede, they obtain rattles and other means for making frightful noises; thus prepared, they approach as near the herds as possible without being seen, and suddenly, with their horses at full speed, rush in among them, making the most hideous and unearthly screams and noises to terrify them, and drive them off before their astonished owners are able to rally and secure them. As soon as the animals are started, the Indians divide their party, leaving a portion to hurry them off rapidly, while the rest linger some distance in the rear, to resist those who may pursue them.

Fording Rivers

"Many streams that the prairie traveler encounters are broad and shallow, and flow over beds of quicksand, which in seasons of high water, become boggy, and then are exceedingly difficult to cross. On arriving upon the bank of a river of this character which has not recently been crossed, the condition of the quicksand may be determined by sending an intelligent man over the fording-place, and, should the sand not yield under his feet, it may be regarded as safe for animals or wagons. Should it, however, prove soft and yielding, it must be thoroughly examined, and the best track selected. This can be done by a man on foot, who will take a number of sharp sticks long enough, when driven into the bottom of the river, to stand above the surface of the water. He starts from the shore, and with one of the sticks and his feet tries the bottom in the direction of the opposite bank until he finds the firmest ground, where he plants one of the sticks to mark the track. A man incurs no danger in walking over quicksand providing he step rapidly, and he will soon detect the safest ground. He then proceeds, planting his sticks as often as may be necessary to mark the way, until he reaches the opposite bank. The ford is thus determined, and if there are footmen in the party, they should cross before the animals and wagons, as they pack the sand, and make the track more firm and secure."

COMANCHE LODGE

Indians

"It is highly important that parties making expeditions through an unexplored country should secure the services of the best guides and hunters, and I know of none who are superior to the Delaware and Shawnee Indians. They are intelligent, brave, reliable, and in every respect well qualified to fill their positions. They are endowed with those keen and wonderful powers in woodcraft which can only be acquired by instinct, practice, and necessity.

"The Delawares are but a minute remnant of the great Algonquin family, whose early traditions declare them to be the parent stock from which the other numerous branches of the Algonquin tribes originated. And they are the same people whom the first white settlers found so numerous upon the banks of the Delaware. When William Penn held his council with the Delawares upon the ground where the city of Philadelphia now stands, they were as peaceful and unwarlike in their habits as the Quakers themselves. They had been conquered by the Iroquois and were forced to forego the use of arms; but after they moved west, beyond the influence of their former masters, their naturally independent spirit revived. They are not clannish in their dispositions like most other Indians, nor by their habits confined to any given locality, but are found as traders, trappers, or hunters among most of the Indian tribes inhabiting our continent. Some even live with the Mormons in Utah. In 1859 the Shawnees had been associated with the Delawares for 185 years. They intermarry and live as one people. Their present places of abode (1859) are upon the Missouri River, near Fort Leavenworth, and in the Choctaw Territory, upon the Canadian River, near Fort Arbuckle. They are familiar with many of the habits and customs of their palefaced neighbors, and some of them speak the English language, yet many of their native characteristics tenaciously cling to them.

"The Indians living between the outer white settlements and the nomadic tribes of the Plains form intermediate social links in the chain of civilization. The first of these occupy permanent habitations, but the others, although they cultivate the soil, are only resident while their crops are growing, going out into the prairies after harvest to spend the winter in hunting. Among the former may be mentioned the Cherokees, Creeks, Choctaws, and Chickasaws, and of the latter the Shawnees, Delawares and Kickapoos who are perfectly familiar with the use of the rifle.

The Wild Tribes of the West
Indian Fighting

"These tribes are very different in their habits from the natives that formerly occupied the country bordering upon the Atlantic coast. The Atlantic coast Indians lived permanently in villages, where they cultivated the soil, and never wandered very far from them. They did not use horses, but always made their war expeditions on foot, and never came into action unless they could screen themselves behind the cover of trees. The prairie tribes have no permanent abiding places; they never plant a seed, but roam for hundreds of miles in every direction over the plains. They are perfect horsemen and seldom go to war on foot. Their attacks are made in the open prairies, and when unhorsed, they are powerless.

"It is highly important to every man passing through a country frequented by Indians to know some of their habits and customs so as to distinguish the friendly and unfriendly tribes.

"Almost every tribe has its own way of constructing its lodges, encamping, making fires, its own style of dress, by some of which peculiarities the experienced frontiersman can generally distinguish them.

"The Osages, for example, make their lodges in the shape of a wagontop, of bent rods or willows covered with skins, blankets or the bark of trees. The Kickapoo lodges are made in an oval form, something like a rounded hay-stack, of poles set in the ground, bent over, and united at top; this is covered with cloths or bark. The Witchetaws, Wacos, Towackanies, and Tonkowas erect their hunting lodges of sticks put up in the form of the frustum of a cone covered with brush. All of these tribes leave the frame-work of their lodges standing when they move from camp to camp, and this, of course, indicates the particular tribe that erected them. The Delawares and Shawnees plant two upright forked poles, place a stick across them, and stretch a canvas covering over it. The Sioux, Cheyennes, Blackfeet and some other tribes of the plains make use of

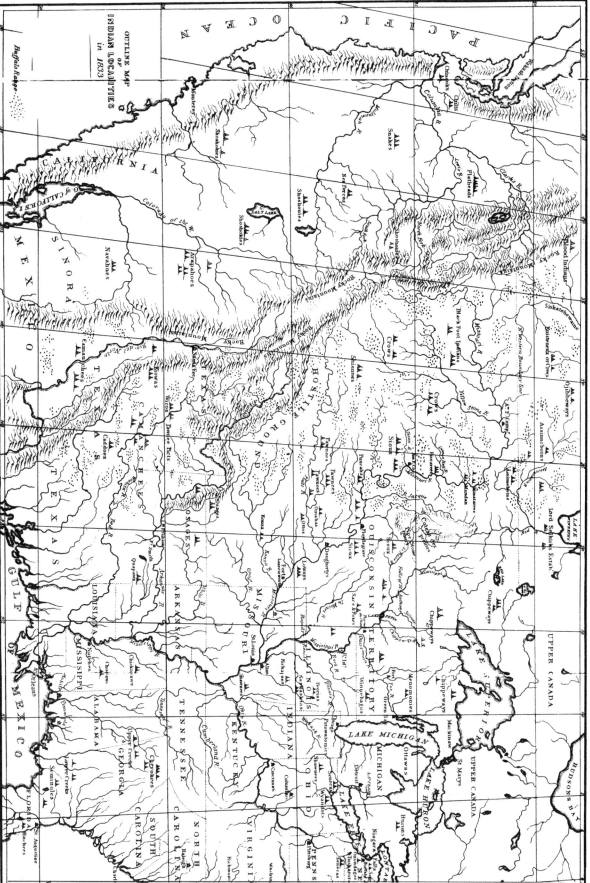

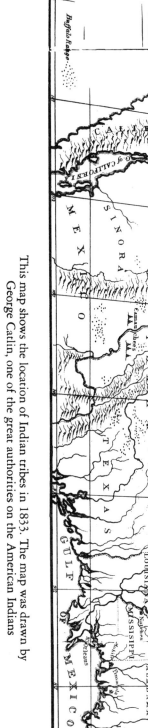

This map shows the location of Indian tribes in 1833. The map was drawn by George Catlin, one of the great authorities on the American Indians

the Comanche lodge. The Sioux, Cheyenees and Blackfeet as well as the Comanches are all unfriendly tribes of the Prairie.

Indian Fighting

"The military system, as taught and practiced in the U.S. Army up to the time of the Mexican War, was without doubt, efficient and well adapted to the art of war among civilized nations, but not so with the Indians. The vast expanse of desert territory that has been annexed to our domain within the last few years is peopled by numerous tribes of marauding savages, who are mounted upon fleet and hardy horses, making war the business and pastime of their lives. Their tactics are such as to render the old system of warfare useless. Today we must act against any enemy who is here today and there tomorrow; who at one time is heard upon the headwaters of the Arkansas, and when next heard from is in the very heart of Mexico; an enemy who is everywhere without being anywhere, who assembles at the moment of combat and vanishes whenever fortune turns against him. This enemy leaves his women and children far distant from the theater of hostilities, and has neither towns or supplies to defend, derives his food and supplies from the country in which he operates, and is not encumbered with the baggage wagons or packtrains. This enemy comes into action only when it suits his purposes, and never without the advantage of numbers or position. With such an enemy as the Indian, the science of war as known by civilized nations loses much of its importance.

"Our little army, scattered as it has been over the vast area of our possessions, in small garrisons of one or two companies each, has seldom been in a position to act on the offensive against these marauders. The morale of our troops has been seriously damaged.

"No people, probably, on the face of the earth entertain a higher appreciation for the deeds of a daring and successful warrior, than the North American Plains Indians. A young man is never considered worthy to occupy a seat in council until he has encountered an enemy in battle; and he who can count the greatest number of scalps is the most highly favored by his tribe. This idea is started early in life. It is not surprising that the young warrior often is anxious to attack the white settlers and these young braves should, therefore, be closely watched when encountered on the Plains.

"A small number of white men, in traveling upon the Plains, should not allow a party of strange Indians to approach them."

KEEP AWAY!

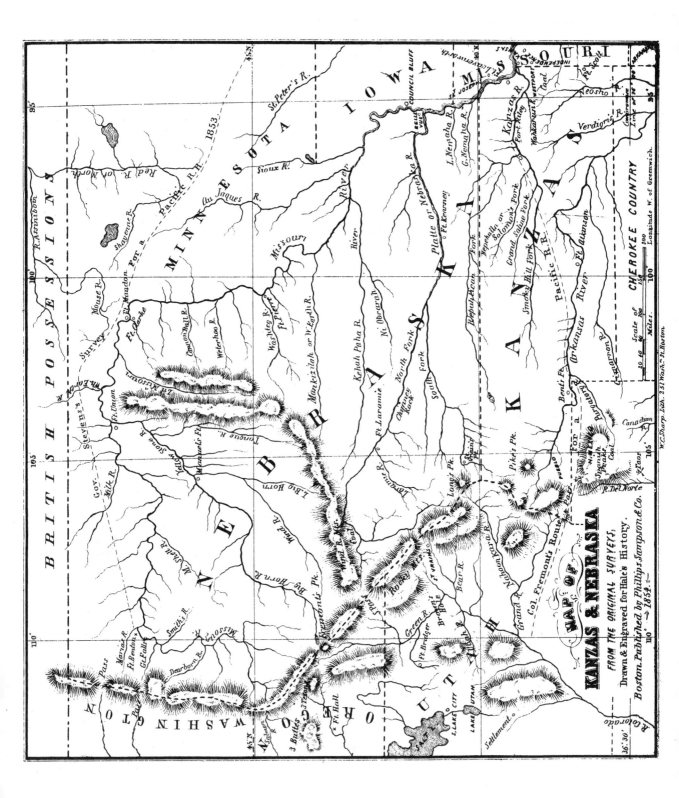

46

Nebraska, Kansas
and Utah Territories

The Nebraska Territory was created by the Kansas-Nebraska Act of May 30, 1854. It was a vast area bounded by the Missouri River on the east, on the south by the Territory of Kansas, on the west by the Rocky Mountains and on the north by the British Possessions, now Canada. The Nebraska Territory today would include the states of Nebraska, North and South Dakota, Montana and Wyoming.

A description of the area of Nebraska through which the wagon trains to California passed is described in *Kanzas and Nebraska,* written by Edward Everett Hale in 1854.

"For about two hundred miles west of the Missouri River, the prairie through which the Nebraska River passes is very rich, and admirably adapted for cultivation. On the northern side it has been less explored than on the southern. On the southern side the regular road from Fort Leavenworth to Fort Kearney passes directly through it. The whole area between the Kanzas and Nebraska Rivers for a distance of 250 miles west of the Missouri River, is soil of loam mixed with gravel; a delightful soil to till, and yielding heavy crops. The valleys are quite well supplied with timber. The country is well watered. In rainy weather the roads now followed become muddy and difficult of travel, but in this respect, it does not differ from any of the prairies of the West. When the season is dry, the ground becomes very firm, and as there are no hills to impede traveling, there is no reason why the best public highways to the western country should not be laid out here.

"The fertile region thus described, nowhere extends more than 250 miles west from the Missouri. A more inhospitable country then begins on both sides of the Nebraska River, which affords pasturage for buffalo and for cattle, but little more which tempts the farmer. It is for a great distance unbroken by hills. For 85 miles west of Fort Kearney the road to Fort Laramie is wholly level. A gentle rolling country then begins. It is upon these dandy plains that the buffalo are now first found by westward emigrants.

"Fort Laramie is 327 miles west of Fort Kearney by the traveled route, and 639 miles from Fort Leavenworth. It is situated on

Laramie's Creek, a rapid stream, about 60 yards wide, with a firm pebbly bottom. There is good grazing on the creek, and pine and cedar wood for the purposes of the fort are procured from the hills on the north of the river, at a distance of about 8 miles.

"Westward of Fort Laramie the country is more broken and hilly. The spurs of the Rocky Mountains are covered with pine forests. The plains beneath are sometimes broken into more uneven surfaces, so as to render traveling more difficult. The route up the North Platte to the Great South Pass is the route followed by all Oregon emigrants and by most of the California parties.

"South of Fort Laramie, a trail known as the Cherokee Trail, crossing the headwaters of the Platte and the various forks of the Kanzas, leads to Pueblo, on the Arkansas, and to Bent's Fort. This trail opens to observation a country mostly barren, sometimes broken by the spurs of water-courses, fresh and green meadows."

The Kansas Territory is described as follows in the book *The States and Territories of The Great West,* written by Jacob Ferris in 1856.

"Kansas Territory lies spread out between the 37th and 40th parallels of north latitude, and from the border of Missouri clear over the Rocky Mountains. The northern boundary consists of a straight line, running due east and west. The southern boundary is directly west along the line of the Indian Territory, and of Texas to New Mexico. The eastern portion is considerably wider than the western. The territory comprises an area of nearly 115,000 square miles.

"The eastern and western extremities of the territory comprise the best lands in Kansas; the middle regions being quite indifferent, and in some places absolutely barren. The finest portions open for settlement in 1856 consist of a strip which extends across the territory contiguous to the Missouri boundary, varying in width from 75 to 180 miles. The bottom lands along the borders of the rivers are equal to any in the world. The upland is composed of a continual succession of ridges and valleys, rising and falling with the regularity of ocean waves. The rivers are belted with timber; but the forests are not so thick, nor the trees so large as those which originally grew in Ohio and New York.

"Further to the westward is a region which affords some advantages for keeping flocks and herds. It consists of long reaches of fertile land lying upon the banks of the tributaries of the Smokey Hill fork of the Kansas River. Beyond this is the vast tract known as the American Desert, extending from Nebraska through Kansas into Texas and New Mexico. There are no small streams, and but few rivers, flowing through this desolate region. The surface is almost a dead, uniform level, sweeping in every direction to the horizon, and is composed of a heavy gray and yellow clay, with not a single tree, only here and there a knob of cactus, and a few blades of bitter grass. The desert terminates to the westward in a range of hills with precipitous sides and flat tops. From the desert-hills to the Rocky Mountains is a beautiful, fertile country, resembling, in many respects, eastern Kansas.

"The Sante Fe road strikes the Arkansas at the Big Bend. The trade with Sante Fe had in 1856 become very important to the economy of the Territory of Kansas.

"The Arapahoe Indians roam over the western part of Kansas. They profess to be friendly to the whites; but the safer policy is to give them a wide berth. The Cheyennes are in alliance with the Arapahoes, professing friendship, but very treacherous. These tribes have control of the Prairies; and they are said to hold there, what in Europe would be called, "the balance of power". These tribes are known to be very numerous, for it is quite common to stumble upon 3 or 4 thousand of them, collected in a single hunting camp. The other aboriginal tribes are the Osages, Kansas and Arkansas numbering about 9,000. The hunting grounds of the Kansas Indians lie around the confluence of the Smokey Hill and Republican Rivers. The name of the tribe is spelled variously — Kanzas, Kansas, Cansas, Konzas, and Consas. The whole Indian population of the territory has been estimated at 25,000." It is interesting that Edward Everett Hale chose the spelling "Kanzas" in his book *Kanzas and Nebraska* from which we quote in this chapter. His reason was that the "z" best expressed the correct sound in the pronunciation of the tribe's name. However the "s" was the more fashionable spelling, and that spelling has survived.

Utah Territory

The most important emigrant routes to California and Oregon went through the Utah Territory. This Territory was bounded on the east by the Kansas and Nebraska Territories, on the south by the

New Mexico Territory, on the north by the Oregon Territory and on the west by the State of California.

Before 1848, the area which later became the Utah Territory, New Mexico Territory and California had belonged to Mexico. In 1848, all that section had passed from the dominion of Mexico to that of the United States. The Mormons, who had settled in Utah in 1847, called a convention which met at Salt Lake City on March 5, 1849. They established a government by the name of the "State of Deseret". Then they elected a delegate to Congress and asked for admission to the United States. Congress, however, did not approve this new state and on Sept. 9th, 1850 passed an act to organize the Territory of Utah and appointed Brigham Young Governor.

There was unrest between the government of the United States and the Mormons because the Mormons believed in poligamy which allows a man to marry more than one wife.

The major settlements in Utah Territory were Salt Lake City which was founded by the Mormons and Fort Bridger which was an important supply point on the overland routes to both California and Oregon. Fort Bridger was named after Col. James Bridger, the oldest mountaineer in that region. Col. Bridger had been engaged in the Indian trade in that area since 1819.

San Francisco

Engraved by Ja: Duthie from a daguerreotype by J.M. Ford.

Montgomery Street, northward from California Street. June 1854.

California

What was the magnet that drew the emigrants to California? What convinced them to give up an often comfortable home in the East and to take an almost four months trip across the great plains, mountains and desert in a covered wagon? They probably knew that such a trip presented great dangers and that some would probably not reach their destination alive, yet tens of thousands made the journey. To find our answer, let us study the history of California beginning in 1847. California had been a part of Mexico until June 14, 1846 when the California Republic (Bear Flag) was raised at Sonoma. The U.S. flag was raised at Monterey July 7, 1846. California was, however, not admitted to the Union as a state until Sept. 9, 1850.

The Annals of San Francisco and The History of California, published in 1855 tells us that in 1847 the population of San Francisco consisted of 321 people. The places in which the inhabitants conducted their business were as follows:

apothecary shops	1	Cigar-maker shop	1	watchmaker	1
blacksmith shops	2	cooper shop	1	stores	8
butcher shops	3	gun smith shop	1	groceries	7
cabinet maker	1	shoemaker shop	1	hotels	2
carpenter shop	1	tailor shop	2	wind-mill	1
horse-mill	1	printing offices	2	bakeries	3

We quote from the *Annals of San Francisco and the History of California".*

"It was in the Spring of 1848 that word was received in San Francisco that gold had been found in large quantities in the foothills of the Sierra Nevada mountains. Small amounts of gold had arrived in San Francisco and visitors from the mines, and some actual diggers arrived to tell about the wonders of the region. As a result of this startling news, the inhabitants of San Francisco, in bands and singly, started deserting their jobs and rushed to the American River and other parts of Sacramento valley where the gold had been discovered. Because of the shortage of labor, wages rose sharply, and soon all business and work, except the most urgent, was forced to be stopped. Seamen deserted from their ships and

WAGONS ARRIVE AT THE UPPER SACRAMENTO

soldiers from their barracks. Over all the country the excitement was the same. Neither threats, punishment or money could keep men away from the gold diggings. The great desire to be rich grew into a disease, and the infection spread on all sides. The daily laborer who had worked for a dollar or two a day rushed to the diggings where he could make six or ten times that amount, and might possibly gain a hundred or even a thousand times the sum in one lucky day. The laborers were followed by their employers; and the storekeepers, with everyone leaving, packed up their business stock and followed the crowd to the mines where they were able to sell their old articles to the fortunate diggers, at a rise of five hundred or a thousand percent.

"In the month of May, 1848 at least 150 people had left San Francisco, and every day since was adding to their number. Newspapers ceased publications because of lack of printers. While San Francisco, like so many other parts of the country was being deserted, the neighborhood of the American River was overflowing with people, all busily engaged in gold hunting. By the middle of May, there were estimated to be about 2,000 miners at the American River. In another month they had increased to 3,000 and two months later to 6,000. From that time on the arrival of people was constant. The miners were by no mean exclusively American. There were tame Indians, Mexicans, settlers from Oregon with the usual mixture of Spanish, British, German and French adventurers that had for a long time existed in California. At first the gains of miners, though great, were little compared to what shortly afterwards were collected. A fair average for a miner was 10 to 15 dollars per day, in gold dust. Some lucky miners averaged 100 to 200 dollars per day and some even obtained 500 to 800 dollars per day in gold dust. If, indeed, in many cases, a man with a pick and pan did not easily gather some 30 or 40 dollars in dust per day, he simply moved off to someplace known to be richer. One piece of pure gold weighing 13 pounds was found. Earth dug out of ravines and holes in the sides of mountains, was packed on horses and carried one, two or three miles to the nearest water, to be washed. An average price of this washing dirt was, at one period, so much as $400 a cart load. In one case, five loads of such earth sold for $750, which yielded, after washing $16,000. Individuals made their 5, 10, and 15 thousand dollars in the space of only a few weeks. But these, of course, were extreme cases. Still it is true that a large proportion of the miners were earning such sums as

LASSENS BUTTE, SACRAMENTO VALLEY.

they had never seen in their lives before, and which six months before, would have appeared a fable. But many of the miners became sick from fever and disease as a result of a complete change of diet and habits and the severe kind of labor, to which most had been unaccustomed. No gains could pay a dying man for the fatal sickness caused by his own greed. In the wild race for richess, the invalid was neglected by old comrades still in good health and enjoying the riotous enjoyment of all the pleasures that gold could bestow.

"Provisions and necessities, as might have been expected, soon rose in price enormously. At first the rise was moderate indeed, 400% for flour, and 500% for beef cattle, while other things were in proportion. But these were trifles. The time soon came when eggs were sold at one, two and three dollars a piece; inferior sugar, tea and coffee, at four dollars a pound in small quantities, or, three or four hundred dollars a barrel. Medicines were often a dollar a drop and often ten dollars a pill. Whiskey was sold at various prices, from ten to forty dollars a quart; and wines at about as much per bottle. Picks and shovels ranged from five to fifteen dollars each; and common wooden or tin bowls about half as much. Small gold scales cost from twenty to thirty dollars each. When these prices, the risks of sickness, the discomforts of living and the unusual and severe kind of labor are all balanced against the average gains, it appears that the miners where not really making much money.

"About the end of May, 1848, San Francisco was all but deserted, and it continued so during the whole summer and autumn months. Many ships with valuable cargoes had meanwhile arrived in the bay, but the seamen deserted. The goods, at great expense, had been somehow landed, but there was nobody to take care of them, or remove them from the wharves where they were exposed to the weather. After awhile, the miners came back to their old homes; but most were feeble and without spirit. In San Francisco, as at the mines, the prices of labor and all necessaries rose exceedingly. The common laborer, who had formerly been content with his dollar a day, now proudly refused ten; the mechanic, who had recently been glad to receive two dollars, now rejected twenty for his day's services. It was certainly a great country, there was no mistake about it; and every subject was as lofty, independent, and seemingly as rich as a king."

"By 1853 the population of San Francisco had increased to 50,000 people as compared to the 321 who lived there in 1847. These were broken down as follows: Americans, 32,000; Germans, 5,500; French, 5,000; Spanish, 3,000; Negroes, 1,500 and Chinese, 3,000. About 8,000 of this population were women and 3,000 children; while the great majority of the remainder were men between the ages of twenty and forty. The greatest number of votes at any one election were only 11,000. This is partly explained by the fact that a large portion of the adult males were neither native nor naturalized citizens. San Francisco, during 1853, was particularly improved by the erection of a large number of elegant and substantial fireproof and stone buildings. Such great structures as Armory Hall, the Express building, the Custom-House Block, and many others of nearly as grand a character, cost enormous sums of money to build.

"By 1853 the total population of the state of California was 326,000 persons. They were broken down as follows: Americans, 204,000; Germans, 30,000; French, 28,000 and Spanish, 20,000. There were also 5,000 additional foreigners of white extraction, also 17,000 Chinese; 20,000 Indians and 2,000 Negroes. Of the total population, about 100,000 are believed to be working miners, the remainder forming the population of the different towns and the agricultural districts of the country. It is estimated that there are about 65,000 women in the country and perhaps 30,000 children. In the mining regions, the women are much fewer relatively to the local population than in the towns.

"The quantity of gold produced from the California mines cannot be correctly determined, however, the following figures give some idea:

	Est. gold production		Est. gold production
1848	$ 3,000,000	1851	$60,000,000
1849	25,000,000	1852	63,000,000
1850	40,000,000	1853	65,000,000

"It has been gold, almost alone, which has given an impetus to the progress of California at large, and particularly San Francisco. This is the one great port through which the enormous foreign supplies of provisions and all other kinds of goods pass to the interior, and from whence the payments in gold dust are shipped abroad. Most of the miners reach California by way of San Francisco. Many years hence the fertile and genial California will be a rich and populous country, irrespective entirely of her mineral wealth. San Francisco will then, as now, be the great port of the State, and the center of a vast commerce. The Atlantic and Pacific Railway, which has been discussed for so many years, and which must soon be really set in operation, will increase to an incalculable extent the population and prosperity both of California and San Francisco. By whatever route the proposed railroad communication is made, our city must be the chief terminus on the Pacific". This prediction, written in 1853, has certainly become a fact. Today California is the fastest growing state in the nation and the end of this growth is nowhere in sight.

"The San Franciscans are proud of their noble city that sits enthroned beside calm water, and as Queen of the Pacific receives homage and tribute from all seas and oceans. Richly freighted ships from every land visit her harbor. Her buildings are becoming palaces, and her merchants, princes. Wealth, gayety and luxury characterize her people. She is fast approaching that peculiar and regal character which in days of old was borne by the great maritime cities of the Mediterranean, in more recent times by Venice and Genoa and perhaps at this date by Amsterdam and St. Petersburgh. Like the great mercantile cities of the past, San Francisco may fall in her pride; but centuries shall first pass. She is very young yet, and has a long age of growing grandeur before her. The commerce of the Pacific is only beginning, and with its certain increase will San Francisco certainly wax greater and more marvellous. Her spirit is GO AHEAD! We have seen her, but a few years since, only a barren waste of sand-hills - a paltry village - a thriving little town - a budding city of canvas, then of wood, and next a great metropolis of brick."

Transportation in and out of San Francisco in 1853 was described as follows:

"There are 18 ocean steamers, of which 8 run to Panama, 4 to San Juan del Sud, 2 to Oregon, and 4 to points on the coast of California; and there are 23 river steamers, which ply to different parts on the bay and its tributaries. There is one line of daily stages to San Jose, another to the Red Woods, and one thrice a week to Monterey. There are regular lines of omnibuses on the plank roads, which run to the mission every half hour. There is a magnetic telegraph eight miles in length, from Point Lobos, for reporting vessels; and another, extending altogether upwards of three hundred miles, to Marysville, through San Jose, Stockton and Sacramento. There are 2 great, and some smaller express companies which convey letters and packages to all parts of the Union, and to many foreign countries. The great Atlantic mails leave twice a month, via Panama; and there are daily mails to all places of importance around the bay or on the Sacramento and San Joaquin Rivers. For nearly two months, in the summer of 1853, a weekly mail left for the eastern states, but this, not being sufficiently supported by the government, came abruptly to an end. About 1,000,000 letters were sent during the year to foreign and Atlantic ports.

"The arrivals of ships in the port of San Francisco in 1853 were 1028 vessels, of which 634 were American and 394 were foreign. The quickest passage of the year were made by the *Flying Fish* and the *John Gilpin,* both clipper ships. These were from New York, and arrived in 92 and 97 days respectively. At the close of the year, there were 72 square rigged sailing vessels in the port, consisting of 21 ships, 36 barques, and 15 brigs.

"There were many hazards in traveling by ship to California. One incident was recorded as follows:

'A terrible disaster was the loss of the steamship *Independence.* The ship stuck upon a sunken reef, about a mile from the shore of Margarita Island, off the coast of Lower California. At this time it was discovered that the vessel was on fire. The people, who had hitherto been quiet, now lost all control of themselves; and many in a frantic state leaped overboard. The crew and passengers amounted to four hundred and fourteen persons; and of this number nearly two hundred perished".

"But the lure of great wealth and luxury and the prosperity of California was the magnet that drew the settlers, most by overland travel and some by ship, despite all of the many hardships along the way."

SAN FRANCISCO IN 1854
From the head of Sacramento St.

SAN FRANCISCO, FROM THE BAY, IN 1847

61

INDEX

INDEX